TOUCH

FARRAR,

STRAUS AND

GIROUX

NEW YORK

TOUCH

HENRI

COLE

Farrar, Straus and Giroux

18 West 18th Street, New York 10011

Distributed in Canada by D&M Publishers, Inc.

Printed in the United States of America

First edition, 2011

Library of Congress Cataloging-in-Publication Data

Cole, Henri.

    Touch / Henri Cole.— 1st ed.

    p. cm.

    ISBN 978-0-374-27835-9 (cloth : alk. paper)

    I. Title.

PS3553.O4725T68 2011

811'.54—dc22

                    2011000757

Designed by Quemadura

www.fsgbooks.com

1 3 5 7 9 10 8 6 4 2

FOR JOHN M. MAZZULLO

(WHO LOOKED, LISTENED, FELT)

CONTENTS

|

II

III

Don't be an open book.

MOTHER

ASLEEP IN JESUS AT REST

(gravestone epitaph)

Their names were Victoria, Ebbenezer, Noah,
                    Fannie, Travis, Alex, Pleasant,
William Christmas, and Jane.
    Like father, they labored in exchange for small wooden houses.
Breaking even was a feat.
                    Things were settled when the crops were in.
They were my ancestors and lived along the Pee Dee River,
                    under tupelo, oak, and gum,
where wolves made dens
                    ("You could smell dem wolves!").
According to the Census, they were mulatto
                    (Spanish *mulato*, small mule).
Women died of uremic poisoning.
                    Children were stillborn.
Those that lived were sprinkled on their foreheads
                    and went to Sunday school,
taught by Mrs. Lillian Ingram,
                    in Wolf Pit Township, North Carolina.
One of them wrote a poem:
        "There in the boughs, in a tiny nest, are three baby birds

[3]

with mouths opened wide."

                        When I was born,
I weighed nine pounds of flesh.

                             Mother's hair fell down
the back of her long neck.

                                Tears ran out of her eyes like animals.
Fragrant convolutions from her insides

                                   filled the room with the strife of love.
Daddy was on a tour of duty.

                        "Remember you got a father," he used to say.
"You weren't born by yourself."

SOLITUDE: THE TOWER

Long ago, I lived at the foot of the mountains,

where my parents lived when they were young.

Nearby, there was a daffodil farm, which I bicycled past

each day on my way to the supermarket.

Occasionally, there were earthquakes, but no one noticed.

At my desk, words and phrases grew only slowly,

like the embedded or basal portion of a hair,

tooth, nail, or nerve. As I looked at the empty page—

seeing into love, seeing into suffering,

seeing into madness—my head ached so,

dear reader, emotions toppling me in one

direction, then another, but writing this now,

sometimes in a rush, sometimes after drifting thought,

I feel happiness, I feel I am not alone.

SHRIKE

How brightly you whistle, pushing the long, soft

feathers on your rump down across the branch,

like the apron of a butcher, as you impale a cricket

on a meat hook deep inside my rhododendron.

Poor cricket can hardly stand the whistling,

not to speak of the brownish-red pecking

(couldn't you go a little easy?), but holds up

pretty good in a state of oneiric pain.

Once, long ago, when they were quarrelling about money,

Father put Mother's head in the oven.

"Who are you?" it pleaded from the hell mouth.

Upstairs in the bathroom, I drank water right out of the tap,

my lips on the faucet. Everything was shaking and bumping.

Earth was drawing me into existence.

SUNFLOWER

When Mother and I first had the do-not-

resuscitate conversation, she lifted her head,

like a drooped sunflower, and said,

"Those dying always want to stay."

Months later, on the kitchen table,

Mars red gladiolus sang *Ode to Joy*,

and we listened. House flies swooped and veered

around us, like the Holy Spirit. "Nature

is always expressing something human,"

Mother commented, her mouth twisting,

as I plucked whiskers from around it.

"Yes, no, please." Tenderness was not yet dust.

Mother sat up, rubbed her eyes drowsily, her breaths

like breakers, the living man the beach.

CHERRY BLOSSOM STORM

A mother is a mother still,
The holiest thing alive.
COLERIDGE,
"The Three Graves"

"Draping my body in the usual sterile manner,

they placed me in a supine position and adequate

general anesthesia was obtained. Then a collar incision

was made at the base of my neck and the strap muscles

incised, the dissection continuing sharply over

both my lobes as inferior vessels and veins

were isolated, litigated, and divided, the cut surfaces

like a cherry blossom storm, except for a small amount

of beefy red identified at the pole. Awakening later,

I heard a voice muttering: *Don't worry about adultery*

(he sleeps in a different room). Don't go down after

midnight. Don't take tranquilizers. Don't love. Don't hate.

Sometimes, the paralysis of a soul awakens it. Sometimes,

awful things have their own kind of beauty."

MECHANICAL SOFT

Walking yesterday in the cold, bright air,

I encountered fifteen horses marching

in a phalanx down the avenue. Long before

they were visible, I heard their shoes striking

the pavement, as language is sometimes audible

before sense arrives. I loved how the wind played

with their long, brushed tails. Though in a faraway

place, I was not a stranger. Mother is dying,

you see, and proximity to this death makes me

nostalgic for the French language. I am not

a typical son, I suppose, valuing happiness,

even while spooning mechanically soft pears—

like light vanishing—into the body whose tissue

once dissolved to create breast milk for me.

GREBE

Faraway sibling, speak for me from your leafy islet inside the forest

where water oozes up from the earth like gems.

I could have been you

sitting placidly day after day on your treasure,

scarcely turning your neck to observe your companion's steadfast

    silvery presence

as he alights and sits beside you in his vigil.

You, who are so sure of your life

in the bough-strangled world men cut back continually,

speak for me, horizon-gatherer, since I cannot see

further than my human eyes allow.

Nobody nearby is aware of your secrets —

not even the Sunday fisherman or the black drummer

with his tom-tom —

in this place of echoes, which was once a savannah.

The world isn't any more timeworn or significant than your egg.

Speak, for I cannot speak for you.

I have no feathers and cannot even distinguish

the blackness of the water from the green.

CLAIRE MALROUX

(translated from the French with the author)

DOLPHINS

The dolphins seem happy—lying on their spines,

showing us their gleaming underparts—as the trainer

rubs their cheeks and makes them chatter loudly.

When she floats on her back, they push her with their snouts,

as if through a Tiepolo sky, and the children shriek gaily,

deranging my senses.

                  Recently, among Mother's things, I found this:

"I am afraid of him. He need psychiatric care. He lead me

to believe strange things. He ignores me, threats me.

Very mean. He want to know about insurance."

Here, amid the screamers, loyalty and love have not

been supplanted by trouble and strife. What shields

the dolphins from implacable aloneness? Why do their souls

have no knowledge of their insignificance? How far off

the modern world seems. Beauty remains unshattered.

MOSQUITO MOTHER

You gave me a nice bite; I hope I didn't rip your wing off,

pushing you away. We were sitting by the window;

outside, there was rain on steroids. Your voice was so funny—

up, down; soft, loud—but distant, I thought, reading

my magazine. Then I felt your subtle knife touching me,

as if I were just some part of the scenery, and we sat

like that a long time, your moist red crown all shiny,

as if from effusions: milk, blood, tears, urine, semen.

Tell me, was I happier there in my loneliness,

you feeding on my arm (*Let go of the spirit departed*),

emotion dripping liquid morphine through me (*Nobody there*),

as when—poem, rope, torture—I couldn't look at the corpse

in the coffin with eyes closed (*Continue your life*)?

It was a subtle knife, too, cutting lipid yellow, until I pushed it away.

FLYING THINGS

Now the spell

has broken,

the bleeding and

coalescing begun,

each day

soft and hard,

cold and warm,

nurturing and distant,

as the cold rain

gives a ghostly aura,

wet-on-wet,

to everything,

moth, squirrel, bee,

fly, and bat providing

occasional reverberations

from the earth,

which soon will be

draped and piled

into abstraction,

as each snowfall—

like linen unfolded,

conjuring the domestic—

forces us inward

into fraught territories

of self and family,

instead of out into waves

at the beach or furrows

in the bronzing garden.

Fold one thousand

paper cranes on the kitchen table

and the spirits will cure you,

a friend once advised,

a thousand crane constructions

to complement, sustain,

and nurture me

when the multi-breasted

"good mother" is gone,

and the art of life

becomes, mostly,

the art of avoiding pain,

so the ceremonial

folding goes on,

each bird folded

and sewn to another,

beak to tail.

IMMORTAL

With the press of a button,

she appears out

of darkness, sitting

with one ankle

over the other,

in a woven dress

and sandals,

traces of coca leaf

still on her lips,

her hair braided finely,

with a wrinkle in one cheek

where her shawl

touched it. Sometime

after her sacrifice,

lightning probably

burned her body,

leaving the marks.

Fifteen maybe,

well nourished, with blood

still in her heart,

she sits in an

acrylic cylinder

at a temperature of zero,

as she did for five

hundred years

in an underground

niche, after drinking

maize beer

and falling asleep,

then freezing.

A plaque states:

According to beliefs,

children do not die
but join ancestors
on the mountaintop.

"She doth not sleep,"
I thought, years later,
kneeling with my
eyes closed beside
Mother's coffin.

"Look, Henri, isn't she beautiful!"
my aunt exclaimed,
but I couldn't.
I don't need to know
what I already know.

DEAD MOTHER

All of life was there—love, death, memory—

as the eyes rolled back into the wrinkled sleeve

of the head, and five or six tears—profound,

unflinching, humane—ran out of her skull,

breathtakingly heroic, and tenderness (massaging

the arms, sponging the lips) morphed into a dog

howling under the bed, the bruised body that

had carried us, splaying itself now, not abstract,

but symbolic, like the hot-water bottle,

the plastic rosaries, the shoes in the wheelchair

("I'm ready to stretch out"), as dents and punctures

of the flesh—those gruesome flowers—a macabre tumor,

and surreal pain, changed into hallowed marble,

a lens was cleared, a coffer penetrated.

BROOM

A starkly lighted room with a tangy iron odor;

a subterranean dankness; a metal showerhead hanging from the

ceiling;

a scalpel, a trocar, a pump; a white marble table; a naked, wrinkled

body faceup on a sheet, with scrubbed skin, clean nails,

and shampooed hair; its mouth sewn shut, with posed lips,

its limbs massaged, its arteries drained, its stomach and intestines

emptied;

a pale blue sweater, artificial pearls, lipstick, and rouge;

hands that once opened, closed, rolled, unrolled, rerolled, folded,

unfolded,

turned, and returned, as if breathing silver, unselfing themselves now

(very painful); hands that once tore open, rended, ripped,

served, sewed, and stroked (very loving), pushing and butting now

with all their strength as their physiognomy fills with firming fluid;

hands once raucous, sublime, quotidian—now strange, cruel, neat;

hands that once chased me gruesomely with a broom, then brushed

my hair.

TOUCH

In a hospital morgue,

I lay in a pine box

propped up in a simple tiled room

with a curtain for privacy

that blew open when each guest

entered the chapel.

I wore an ivory silk shirt

and held a pink rose.

White satin covered me to the waist

and was crudely stapled

around the edges of the coffin.

Then some morgue-men nudged the lid into place,

tightened the screws with a ratchet brace

that made a shrieking sound,

melted wax over the screw-heads to seal them,

and nailed a crucifix to the place

over my mouth,

or what had been my mouth.

On a hillside,

they lowered me with ropes into rock,

and those who looked

glimpsed the buffed star on your coffin glinting in the black,

instead of a sea of skulls.

Then I lay down beside you,

dissolving loneliness,

and the white maggots wriggled.

As the preacher spoke,

no one seemed to hear him,

tamping their eyes, touching one another.

He wore a long, black hooded robe

and carried a staff,

at the top of which two snakes

hissed at one another.

He crumbled dry soil over us.

He seemed emotional.

Remember the canaries

in the utility room off the kitchen,

a mother and her offspring

with yellow bodies and tick marks?

Remember how they sang with their beaks closed

when we set them free each night,

listening and watching

as they circled overhead

in the bright lights that imitated daybreak?

Remember the notes that resembled bubbling water?

What a fine performance they gave!

Though they didn't know where they were going,

they made their prettiest song of all.

II

His beak is focussed; he is preoccupied,

looking for something, something, something.

ELIZABETH BISHOP

"Sandpiper"

HENS

It's good for the ego, when I call and they come

running, squawking, and clucking, because it's feed time,

and once again I can't resist picking up little Lazarus,

an orange-and-white pullet I adore. "Yes, yes, everything will be

okay," I say to her glaring mongrel face. Come September,

she'll begin to lay the blue-green eggs I love poached.

God dooms the snake to taste nothing but the dust

and the hen to 4,000 or so ovulations. Poor Lazarus,

last spring an intruder murdered her sisters and left her

garroted in the coop. There's a way the wounded

light up a dark rectangular space. Suffering becomes

the universal theme. Too soft, and you'll be squeezed;

too hard, and you'll be broken. Even a hen knows this,

posing on a manure pile, her body a stab of gold.

TAXIDERMIED FAWN

When a soft projectile hits a fixed obstacle,

soft comes out of it badly. Over there,

in the bedroom, that's a fawn.

Salt, blood, and saliva are gone now.

Sleep and death have transported the lithe body,

folded legs, and tiny bumps on the head.

A minor smear on the white spots is the only

evidence of a violent passage from bridal innocence

to the whiteness of death, which is the absence

of everything, and, in the end, all there really is.

It's dark now, pitch dark. When you walk

through a beam of light, bending your head back,

I'm not scared. I think, *Well, what a pretty body,*

and then I remember you are dead.

ULRO

It's a myth, the push-pull thing, the polarity stuff,

the of-two-minds / left-brain-right-brain discussions.

The world is nothing but the scraping of a donkey,

so he took three Percocet and put a gun to his head.

Last night, I dreamed so strongly about it—

the people touching his arms and legs to see

if they should be calling an ambulance,

the unfamiliar faces right in front of his nose.

Who does not believe his lice are hoofed animals?

Who does not win renown by committing an atrocity?

Cigarettes, love, work, liquor, brooding, despair—

one thing not controlled can destroy a life. Jesus,

I miss him. Why did his eyes have no veils?

Why was the salt of wisdom no good to him?

RAIN AND MOUNTAINS

Sitting on a ledge,

observing the landscape

below, she admires

the proportional

beauty

of the sycamores,

spires, and greens,

but the air smells ornery,

and she is distracted

by a vibration.

She wants to wash

her hands but cannot.

All things might

change but do not.

Plagued by uneasy thoughts,

she wishes she'd

taken the drugs.

It's as if her head were

partially blown off.

Who will find her?

The view across

the valley reveals

an electrical storm coming in,

squeezing the clouds,

tearing them asunder.

Long ago,

her parents nuzzled her,

murmuring, *My love*,

but now her eyes

are salt-choked,

and a fragrance

blows from the river,

as daylight topples over,

darkness coming

suddenly in the North.

WAKING

There was a parade of humans, mostly naked:
a bishop holding a crosier; a drinker with a protruding nose;
a man fighting a bird, mounting it, pulling on its beard;
a granny dragging a money bag; an adolescent boy
with a snake coiling his neck. Their bodies were gaunt
and under their feet yawned the Mouth of Hell.
There were sixteen coffins, too, with people
climbing out of them, including a child, who sat dazed
on a little one, but the scene didn't seem gruesome,
because there were trumpets blowing, making thought
almost impossible. Two of the sinners were trying
to escape, clinging to one of the Elect, who kicked
them back. Everyone clenched his fists. Everyone
held his head, as if it were going to roll off.

Supporting this scene was a pair of Enormous Hands,
expressing a mood of Agony, and a voice muttering
platitudes—*The ways of God are strange.*
Here, where suffering had the nature of Infinity,

my soft voice and demeanor were useless.
In a pint jar, I carried a cremated friend,
like flesh scraped from a cistern.

                         Then I awakened,
and I was still wearing my red pajamas. The wind
was blowing, touching everything in the room.
A barge full of trash pushed another barge up the middle
of the river, creating brown waves that broke against
the mighty purple rhododendrons on the riverbank,
which seemed to say: *There is nothing to fear.* Last week,
it was the iris and before that the honeysuckle.

P I G

Poor patient pig—trying to keep his balance,

that's all, upright on a flatbed ahead of me,

somewhere between Pennsylvania and Ohio,

enjoying the wind, maybe, against the tufts of hair

on the tops of his ears, like a Stoic at the foot

of the gallows, or, with my eyes heavy and glazed

from caffeine and driving, like a soul disembarking,

its flesh probably bacon now tipping into split

pea soup, or, more painful to me, like a man

in his middle years struggling to remain

vital and honest while we're all just floating

around accidental-like on a breeze.

What funny thoughts slide into the head,

alone on the interstate with no place to be.

BLOODSTAINS

Elephants are not supposed to saunter down city streets,

with bar girls ducking under their bellies, or stumble

into the gutter knocking off side-view mirrors as I sit nursing a scotch,

asking myself: What is this earth? What is this planet

or this body in which I live, its Y-chromosome forking, mutating,

tracing back to a time in this place where men and women—

shoeless, heads shaved, eyes pink-stained—were confined

before being transplanted to the Americas? The violence

of it is painful. We all come from our mothers' bellies.

We all have hope in our veins. We don't want history to forget us,

but the dead look after the afterwards. Gazing into the bar mirror,

my brow and jaw less pronounced than my father's,

weary at the neck, I want to be real, to think, to live.

I want to press my face up to the glass and climb out.

HAIRY SPIDER

There's nothing like a big, long-legged spider to embody
the mind's life-giving power, especially when her babies
run up and stroke her face (if she has a face). Soon it will storm
and all of them will drown. Still, I love to watch their web changing,
like this year's words for this year's language, not didactic,
but affective, while absorbing the secret vibrations from the world,
and I love it when she climbs across clear water and drags
some horsefly back, like Beelzebub, to her silk coffer.
There's something unsettling happening, I know, but it tests
the connections between everything. Can she see if I am climbing,
I wonder, or kneeling down here on the dock, day after day,
when it's time for reading and writing again, and a hairy spider—
ingenious, bashful, insolent, laborious, patient—observes
a man no different than a lily, a worm, a clod of clay?

LAST WORDS

She wore blue slacks with a white blouse

and ate a meal of asparagus with strawberries.

When an officer asked if she had anything

to say, she replied, "No, sir," then closed her eyes,

as they strapped her shaved head to the chair.

A handful of protesters stood at the road,

where a witness reported what had gone off without

a hitch (except for a little white smoke that came

out of her right ankle where an electrode was

fastened) as 2,300 watts of electricity shot

through her. "The dead are content," he asserted.

Then a white hearse appeared at the prison gates,

carrying the body of the laughing, girlish nail salon

operator who'd put a pickax in her husband.

L E G E N D

On a rise overlooking a valley

                circled by blue metrical mountains,

where the river source lies,

          a collection of shabby dwellings around a church

became a town on a hill

        with a single gate, a few high windows, a deep moat,

and thick perimeter walls

       in which twenty or thirty families lived, self-sufficient,

the women spinning wool,

          the men hunting with nets and falconry,

until, without provocation,

         their Lord was murdered in his sleep.

It takes a special charisma for one man to say to another,

            "Go forth, kill and be killed."

Soon there were only a gaunt, arched pig

           grubbing among the stones,

a few cocks, and a weary hen.

         When an earthquake made the towers sway,

a young heir rebuilt them.

      Away with the battlements, away with the drawbridges.

Ditches and moats filled in and planted.

           Windows and terraces opened.

The chapel renovated.

        Flocks of sheep contributed wool and soft cheeses.
Oxen harrowed the fields.

         Lives of the inhabitants prospered for a time,
while on another perch, a battlement rose,

          and a warlord with a little white goat watched.

THE FLAGELLATION

(Piero della Francesca, The Flagellation,
Urbino, Galleria Nazionale delle Marche)

Soon they'll knock nails into him, but first there's this,

a lesson in perspective with two worlds coming together:

one gloomy and transgressive, let's call it super-real,

a world behind this world, in which a man is tied to

a column— his hair and beard unkempt, his body raw,

though not bleeding—muttering, "I am afraid to fall down,

but I will not be dominated"; the other world is surreally

calm, with saturated colors and costumes of the day,

a youth's head framed by a laurel tree, nothing

appearing larger than it is, so the eyes drift back

to the deviant, the melancholic, the real, emotion

punching through the rational—like mother cat with five

kittens in her tummy purring in my lap now—

as a man for his beliefs receives blow after blow.

QUAI AUX FLEURS

I want to just keep on smearing butter

& jam on toast with a blunt knife

and licking foam from my espresso cup,

while listening to Lizzy and Tricia practice French,

but I'm a realist. Even the songbirds have levels

of mercury in their blood and feathers. Somewhere,

in the brightness against a wall, a soldier crouches—

sand in his hair, juices dripping from his body.

Here there is joy, like a hole with greenness coming

out of it, but there night pushes against the cylinder

of his gun. He probably has a knife, too, in the presence

of the incomprehensible, thrusting his belly

to the ground, feeling the strangeness throb in his blood

as he touches the scope to his cheek.

ORANGE HOLE

The horses were so beautiful but the people

ugly. Why is that? Both seemed perfectly alive.

Both seemed to want to do what was asked of them

as bullets snapped hitting branches and rocks,

and a blast wave blew everything down.

I crouched against a boulder looking for safety,

returning fire, everything in dreamy slow motion,

orange smoke drifting out of the misty hole,

introducing the idea of beauty as a salve

and of aesthetics making something difficult accessible.

Alone in that box of crisscrossing lead—

my ears ringing, my skin pouring sweat—

I missed you. But it was a rather pleasant feeling

being waited for. I thought, God must be happy.

SLEEPING SOLDIERS

(from a newspaper photograph)

Grow old. Buy a house. Have a baby. Love someone.

Sometimes there are substitutions. A historical torque

pulls us away. A dearest beloved—in a harbor, trench, or house—

lies begging for morphine (just fucking do it,

the best place is in the neck!). Runaway? Fight the power?

"Oh, she was a good girl." "His daddy was enlisted.

The apple don't fall far from the tree."

                                      After operations South,

the soldiers are sleeping now, in various postures of weariness,

on an oriental carpet—knees tucked into their chests,

arms touching one another—everything all interwoven,

like something abstract deep within us—

a soul, maybe—bare-knuckled, but delicate, too,

like a scissored-out black cameo held up

to the light before it is cut deeper.

to be free

Is often to be lonely

W. H. AUDEN

"In Memory of Sigmund Freud"

BATS

Each night they come back, chasing one another

among the fronds after gorging on papayas,

to drink from the swimming pool. With my sleep-

stiffened bones, I like to watch them, careening

into the bright pool lights, spattering the walls with pulp

and guano, like graffiti artists. Sometimes, when they meet,

they hit one another's furred wings—*Love thy neighbor*

like thyself—and then soar off again to drink

more bleached water. Sometimes, it seems as if

they are watching me, like a Styrofoam head

with a wig on it. "The patient reports that he has

been lonely all his life," one screams to the other.

I can hardly stand it and put my face in my hands,

as they dive to-and-fro through all their happiness.

SEAWEED

I love the green and brown seaweed
floating freely on the surface of the water,
like a Jackson Pollock, or an enormous bed
in which the world is no longer a place
of rigid structures. I feel drawn to it but also
to the sea with all its gigantic beauty pushing
against us and below. I want to look at you
but I do not. The edge of the beach brims
with light that glides down around our legs
and then down into the folded depths,
from which the waves erupt, toppling us suddenly
into their undulating plash, connecting—
over a vast terrain of ditches—the salt of sweat,
the salt of tears, and the salt of the sea.

PASSION

Climbing around the immense bronze lap

of Buddha, wearing only briefs, short white robes,

and zori, the priests appear on the verge of song,

mopping and washing his big hypnotized eyes,

the thick, caressable curls of his hair,

and the outstretched hand urging, "Here I am,

I am a hand," strengthening a feeling of being

in myself, as I wander around below,

inhaling the odor of it, and the summer sky

divides and glows, releasing big sparks of rain

that seem almost to bruise me, as I swallow

the hot mouthfuls, thinking, *Our love has ended.*

We only have a little time, darling. Let's read,

swim, and sleep in one another's arms.

ONE ANIMAL

Do not show how jealous you are. Do not
show how much you care. Do not think the bunch
of flowers in his hand connects the hand to you.
Do not close your eyes and kiss the funny
lips. Do not twist your torso, touching yourself
like a monkey. Do not put your mouth
on the filthy place that changes everything.
Do not utter the monosyllable twice that is
the signature of dogdom. Do not, afterward,
appear mangy with old breath, scrutinizing
every hole. And do not think—touching his hair,
licking, sucking, and being sucked in the same
instant, no longer lonely—that you
are two animals perfect as one.

LAUGHING MONSTER

"Some people take and some people get took,"
my father used to say, and I just ignored him.
After all, he'd wake up and take a swig with his juice.
Years later, I watch you emerge from the bathroom,
having breathed your fix, and wonder what it feels like—
the mild euphoria, the expression of power on your face,
the burst of relaxation—a little mirror to mull over
the question "Who am I and why?" Lunging forward
to assume the positions so imprecise to our natures,
hunting the elusive laughing monster of contentment—
my lips numb from yours (it numbs u if it's real,
it numbs ur throat and nose, and it numbs u inside
if u put it in there)—slovenly, degraded, vain,
I wonder if I am the taker or being took?

SELF-PORTRAIT WITH ADDICT

You won't come to bed because you're

doing amphetamines again. There's no animal

that sleep-deprives itself like the human.

Please, I say, repeating the monosyllable.

Rian-rian, the Chinese dog mutters. *Wan-wan*,

the French. Delta waves (they look like

mountains) indicate the start of deep sleep.

Or is it just the down stroking of love?

There is no place in the world—, oh, never mind.

This morning, my thoughts are disorderly,

like black hairs. Listening to you sleep,

I love the refractive gaze of the eyes.

Tell me, my love, marching forward,

how will I bear the mighty freedom?

QUILT

Little muslin sacks from chewing tobacco,

home-dyed in pink and yellow, pieced as a zigzag—

a lively recycling of materials seen often in the South—

with sturdy stitches and a two-color scheme,

like a temperature chart pulled up around me.

What temperature is Henri, the black sheep,

arriving unexpectedly with a new lover—alcoholic

and impetuous—jolting the rest of the family

into spasms of pity, resentment, and half admiring

amazement at his sheer nerve? I'm sorry I broke

the Ming Dynasty jar and set Poppop's beard on fire.

I could actually be normal if the imagination

(unstable, disquieting, fragile) is the Father penetrating

the Mother and this is my Child-poem.

DOLL

Thrown on the carpet with your legs awry—

broken, scalped, microwaved—a receptacle

of love, you make me think the soul is larger

than the body. He lay like that the last time

I saw him, inhaling powder through a straw.

Studies show monkeys prefer it to the food

in their cages; this happens even when the monkeys

are starving. "You are all darkness," he used to say,

"and I am light." Though I understood this alertness

as compassion, it wasn't.

                  It's March now;

the light is brittle, hard, frozen.

Experience seems to come from a distance.

Waiting for spring thaw, I throw you

in a box with the others.

RESISTANCE

Why didn't I tell you before? I'm telling
you now. I didn't go to him for virtue.
I liked the sound of someone else breathing.
I wanted to know what it felt like, eating honey
like a wasp. "Loser old man u r a cheap cunt,"
he wrote, "I need coke. Unless ur buying,
answer is no." Now, the whole insane,
undignified attempt at loving him is over,
the horrible sticky body that was mine
is mahogany in daylight. I intended to make
a poem about the superiority of language over
brute force, but this came instead: "Sleep sleep sleep,
no more wasting my ass with ur sleep." Still, entering
the room, I felt liquid, my eyes cleared.

AWAY

If I close my eyes, I see you again in front of me,

like light attracting light to itself. I'm standing

in the lake, forming a whirlpool with my arms,

letting the force of atonement pull me into its center

until I cannot any longer hang onto my observations

or any sense of myself, like dust and hydrogen clouds

getting all excited while creating new stars to light

the backyard. How poignantly emptiness cries out

to be filled.

But writing this now, my hand is warm.

The character I call Myself isn't lustful, heavy,

melancholic. It's as if emotions are no longer bodied.

Eros isn't ripping through darkness. It's as if I'm

a boy again, observing the births of two baby lambs.

The world has just come into existence.

BY THE NAME OF GOD, THE MOST
MERCIFUL AND GRACIOUS

My name is —— a student in high school.

It cost me such an effort to look at you.

Me and my family were sleeping when we heard knocking.

My heart was racing. I thought I might die.

Then soldiers entered and commenced searching the house (it was

　　five in the morning).

Any love was a good love, I thought, so I took what I could get.

They tied my brother and father—and my hands—and took us to

　　their quarters.

For a time, the here-and-now of life in the flesh carried us along.

They put bags on our heads in a room containing a vocal device

　　(so big recorder) and rised the voice loudly, then started.

Where does the pain come from? I'm afraid of its power.

They didn't give us food or water except once for two days, pouring

　　cold water on our bodies at night, beating us during the day.

Why should I be afraid to die? I belong to you.

When a soldier kicked me a strong kick on my face, my teeth break.

I love your lips, the spur-of-the-moment statements of revolt. I kiss
  them now.

Also, my down jaw (several fractures).

I cannot command myself before the features of your face.

After, they told me to say I fallen down and no one beated me.

I don't feel guilty. Guilt is a wicked ghost.

Then they transferred me from —— to —— without treatment of
  my wounds.

I feel like a jug in which wine is poured until it overflows.

Now, for eight days, I am in hospital for remedy.

Where does this feeling come from, like sunlight falling through the
  valley, changing everything it touches?

I am from a poor family. I have two brothers, one is a child and the
  other is twenty-five years old, but he suffers from three diseases
  that are kidney, stomach, and wind pipe.

Please pray for me that I will sleep well in this strange city.

He is incapable to work. I also have five sisters.

Forgive me for not understanding compromise is human, extremity
  malign.

After my duration in school, I work as a carrier of pebbles and sand.

I wait for you, like a lamb chewing grass, waiting for his brother.

My father is an old man. The —— took him with my brother, and I

    don't know where are they, or in which detention.

At night, in dream, you come to me and sleep between my legs.

I hope to release in time for my commencement.

I say tender things to you.

Also, to work and help survive my family (my mother and sisters).

Neither of us is surprised.

Be so kind to review my case.

CARWASH

I love the iridescent tricolor slime

that squirts all over my Honda in random

yet purposeful patterns as I sit in the semi-

dark of the "touch-free" carwash with you.

Listening to the undercarriage blast, I think,

"Love changes and will not be commanded."

I smile at the long, flesh-colored tentacles waving

at us like passengers waving good-bye.

Water isn't shaped like a river or ocean;

it mists invisibly against metal and glass.

In the corridor of green unnatural lights

recalling the lunatic asylum, how can I

defend myself against what I want?

Lay your head in my lap. Touch me.

MYSELF DEPARTING

My hair went away in the night while I was sleeping.
It sauntered along the avenue asking, "Why
should I commit myself to him? I have a personality
of my own." Then my good stiff prick went, too.
It opened the window and climbed down the escape,
complaining, "I want to be with someone younger."
The floor was no longer a place for urgent love.
The pretty body I wanted no longer galloped over me,
shouting, "Open, open!" Then fire erupted over
a vast inward terrain that wasn't happiness.
People are always abandoning something; they feel
they haven't been allowed to grow. Though my eyes
leaked, my fingers, cracked from thirst, dried them.
The ring was gone, but the finger lived.

SWIMMING HOLE, BUCK CREEK, SPRINGFIELD, OHIO

Like an echo,

it comes back,

the bend in the creek,

like a uterus'

bleeding flow,

tangible again,

as memory revisits,

with unusual

concreteness,

territories of the past,

rebounding, circulating,

surging, vexing,

panning our naked

bodies—some of us

in the water, loin-deep,

making animal sounds;
some of us out,
wistfully small,
under a depthless sky—
all of us boys still,

like blossoming buds,
bending under
the paw of some
hormonal energy
that lingers now

in memory's tunnel,
like an air prowling
around us, vaguely
ornery, urging:
"Begin what you are,"

though not intended
to belittle me for my
unmasculine traits,

but, instead,

to lift me up,

allowing new light

to enter in, its strong

broad rays in free fall

against my flesh,

as if through blades

of pungent grass,

piercing me

even deeper now, to say,

"Be kind to him,

stranger that he is."

ACKNOWLEDGMENTS

For their encouragement, I am indebted to the editors of the following publications, where these poems, sometimes in different form, were originally published.

Alaska Quarterly Review: "Sunflower"; *The American Scholar*: "By the Name of God, the Most Merciful and Gracious," "Passion," "Seaweed," and "Taxidermied Fawn"; *The Atlantic*: "Hens," "Immortal," "Pig," and "Quai aux Fleurs"; *The Believer*: "Legend"; *The Harvard Advocate*: "Rain and Mountains"; *Harvard Magazine*: "Swimming Hole, Buck Creek, Springfield, Ohio"; *Literary Imagination*: "Mosquito Mother"; *The New Republic*: "Carwash," "Flying Things," and "Orange Hole"; *The New Yorker*: "Shrike"; *The New York Review of Books*: "Laughing Monster," "Mechanical Soft," "One Animal," and "Sleeping Soldiers"; *Poem-A-Day* (Academy of American Poets): "Cherry Blossom Storm"; *Salmagundi*: "Grebe" (translation), "Touch," "Ulro," and "Waking"; *Slate*: "Asleep in Jesus at Rest" and "Dead Mother"; *The Threepenny Review*: "Bats," "Broom," and "The Flagellation"; *West 10th*: "Hairy Spider"

I would also like to record my thanks to the Academy of American Poets, the National Endowment for the Arts, United States Artists, and Wellesley College for awards that were a great help in writing this book.

My thanks also to the Blue Mountain Center, the Tyrone Guthrie Centre, Civitella Ranieri, and the MacDowell Colony for their hospitality and for solitude during residencies.

[67]